金融管理与实务专业
教学标准

THE TEACHING STANDARDS FOR THE PROGRAM OF FINANCIAL MANAGEMENT AND PRACTICE

郭福春　董瑞丽　王德英◎著

中国金融出版社

责任编辑：方　晓
责任校对：张志文
责任印制：陈晓川

图书在版编目（CIP）数据

金融管理与实务专业教学标准（Jinrong Guanli yu Shiwu Zhuanye Jiaoxue Biaozhun）/郭福春，董瑞丽，王德英著．—北京：中国金融出版社，2015.4

ISBN 978－7－5049－7795－3

Ⅰ．①金…　Ⅱ．①郭…②董…③王…　Ⅲ．①金融管理—课程标准—高等职业教育—教学参考资料　Ⅳ．①F830.2－41

中国版本图书馆CIP数据核字（2015）第019476号

出版发行 中国金融出版社
社址　北京市丰台区益泽路2号
市场开发部　（010）63266347，63805472，63439533（传真）
网上书店　http：//www.chinafph.com
（010）63286832，63365686（传真）
读者服务部　（010）66070833，62568380
邮编　100071
经销　新华书店
印刷　三河市利兴印刷有限公司
尺寸　169毫米×239毫米
印张　4.5
字数　70千
版次　2015年4月第1版
印次　2015年4月第1次印刷
定价　22.00元
ISBN 978－7－5049－7795－3/F.7355
如出现印装错误本社负责调换　联系电话（010）63263947
编辑部邮箱：jiaocaiyibu@126.com

前　言

我国高职教育进入内涵建设关键时期，对于专业教学的整体规范和质量标准提出了更高的要求。同时，商业银行等金融机构对于一线从业人员的综合素质要求也日益提高，对金融专业提出了更为系统的教学建设要求。因此，开发兼具国际水准和中国特色的职业教育专业教学标准，就成为提升我国职业教育质量与吸引力的关键。

《金融管理与实务专业教学标准》以商业银行等金融机构一线业务岗位任务分析为起点，以学生职业能力建构过程为主线，根据一线业务岗位的典型流程的主要节点、要素等确立课程开发的整体框架并安排课程内容，强化了学历证书与职业资格证书的对接以及课程结构与职业能力结构的对接，突出了课程体系的职业性和实践性，解决了课程教学与职业能力要求相脱节的难题。

本标准主要是框架性、规范性的专业建设要求，所提出的只是金融专业基本职业能力要求，主要是对本专业相对稳定的基本内容进行了规定，具有较强的开放性和兼容性，各高职院校可根据自身实际在此基础上进行二次开发。

目 录

English Version

一、专业名称与代码

金融管理与实务（620103）

二、学制与学历

学制：三年
学历：专科

三、入学要求

普通高中毕业生/中等职业学校毕业生

四、职业岗位描述

本专业毕业生面向商业银行等金融机构一线业务岗位，能够胜任的初始岗位包括临柜交易、服务营销、业务管理等。

（一）临柜交易

工作项目	工作任务	职业能力
1. 储蓄、出纳业务	1－1 营业前准备	• 能按照相关规定做好网点安全、卫生检查等 • 能按规定摆放营业开始所需用具 • 与业务员办理好钱箱交接，准备开始营业
	1－2 受理审查	• 能和客户进行良好的沟通 • 能审查客户有效证件的真实性

续表

工作项目	工作任务	职业能力
		• 能识别客户存单、存折、支票等支付凭证的真实性 • 能辨认客户签名的准确性 • 能掌握储蓄业务品种的具体规定（包括存期、存款金额起点等） • 能具备良好的职业道德素质
	1-3 现金收付	• 能掌握现金收付的基本原则 • 能熟练点钞 • 能准确鉴别假币
	1-4 记账（录入）	• 能审核凭证要素的合规性 • 能熟练打字（五笔输入法） • 能熟练录入传票（数字键盘的录入） • 能根据不同业务流程进行规范处理
	1-5 复核（授权）	• 能掌握有关法律法规的基本规定 • 能熟悉操作流程 • 能确定客户身份
	1-6 日终业务处理	• 能够熟练整理各种凭证 • 能够严格执行钱箱交接等相关交接制度 • 能够保持高度的风险意识
2. 会计业务	2-1 营业前准备	• 能按照相关规定做好网点安全、卫生检查等 • 能按规定摆放营业开始所需用具 • 能顺利进行业务系统柜员签到
	2-2 开户	• 掌握银行会计基础知识 • 能熟练掌握账户开立的相关规定 • 会审查开户资料及相关证件的真实性、合规性 • 掌握开户申请书的填列，确保信息填列的完整准确 • 会熟练操作开户交易，进行系统操作
	2-3 受理审查票据	• 能掌握《支付结算办法》和《票据法》的相关知识 • 能辨别票据的真伪 • 能掌握票据填写的基本规范 • 能了解客户需要，与客户良好沟通
	2-4 记账（录入）	• 能熟练掌握汉字的录入、数字键盘的录入 • 能掌握《票据法》《支付结算办法》的各项内容

续表

工作项目	工作任务	职业能力
		• 会审查银行汇票、商业承兑汇票、转账支票、汇兑凭证等各项票据业务凭证的真伪、票面要素的合理合规性 • 掌握银行业务的会计基础知识（核算流程、利息计算、风险控制） • 能掌握信贷业务、中间业务的会计操作 • 了解人民银行汇兑汇率及资金清算办法 • 会录入操作
	2－5 复核（授权）	• 能熟练掌握汉字的录入、数字键盘的录入 • 能掌握《票据法》《支付结算办法》的各项内容 • 会审查银行汇票、商业承兑汇票、转账支票、汇兑凭证等各项票据业务凭证的真伪、票面要素的合理合规性 • 掌握银行业务的会计基础知识（核算流程、利息计算、风险控制） • 掌握信贷业务、中间业务的会计操作 • 了解人民银行汇兑汇率及资金清算办法 • 具备一定的把握业务风险的能力 • 会录入操作
	2－6 销户	• 掌握银行会计基础知识 • 能熟练掌握账户销户的相关规定 • 会审查销户资料及相关证件的真实性、合规性 • 掌握销户前的各项审查工作 • 会熟练操作销户交易，进行系统操作 • 掌握人行《账户管理办法》《支付结算办法》等规章制度
	2－7 日终业务处理	• 能进行当天业务凭证的整理、核对工作 • 能进行重要凭证、印章的盘点、入库 • 能正确进行系统签退
3. 银行卡业务	3－1 临柜取现	• 熟练掌握银行卡产品的功能和费用标准 • 能分产品正确审核卡片种类，能识别假卡 • 能判断客户身份证明的真伪，准确识别客户身份 • 能根据业务操作流程进行系统操作 • 掌握超权限时主管授权的操作规定，并正确操作 • 能正确核对客户签字

续表

工作项目	工作任务	职业能力
	3－2 临柜存(还）款	• 熟练掌握银行卡产品的功能和费用标准 • 能熟练识别人民币真伪，识别假币 • 能根据业务操作流程进行操作
	3－3 临柜转账	• 熟练掌握银行卡产品的功能和费用标准 • 能分产品正确审核卡片种类，能识别假卡 • 能判断客户身份证明的真伪，准确识别客户身份 • 能根据业务操作流程进行系统操作 • 掌握超权限时主管授权的操作规定，并正确操作 • 能正确核对客户签字
	3－4 临柜销户	• 能分产品识别卡片的种类 • 能通过系统查询确定客户销户前未了的相关业务，并按规定进行处理 • 能正确进行系统的销户处理 • 能根据风险控制要求收回卡片，并进行账务处理
	3－5 临柜挂失	• 能根据客户要求受理挂失业务 • 能熟练处理挂失交易
	3－6 临柜收单	• 能根据业务规定进行单据正确性的判断 • 能正确核实单据资金的准确性 • 能正确处理收单操作
	3－7 查询及修改客户资料	• 能根据客户要求进行受理 • 能正确进行系统操作
	3－8 申请表受理	• 能正确审核申请表的完整性和准确性 • 能初步根据授信等级判断申请额度
	3－9 客户投诉及咨询	• 能按照客户投诉内容依据业务管理的相关规定进行处理 • 能按照客户咨询内容依据业务管理的相关规定进行处理
	3－10 ATM 清机（不包括清算）	• 能熟练掌握清机处理流程，并正确操作 • 能正确进行 ATM 现金库的操作 • 能处理 ATM 日常性故障
	3－11 特殊业务处理	• 能正确受理银行卡换卡业务，按照规定进行换卡操作 • 能根据银行的授信政策正确处理银行卡临时调额业务 • 能根据风险管理的要求正确受理银行卡账户的冻结和解冻

（二）服务营销

工作项目	工作任务	职业能力
1. 公司金融业务	1－1 确定营销对象	• 能了解各行业现状 • 至少对某一行业特别熟悉
	1－2 调查客户概况、行业地位	• 能进行行业地位分析 • 具备企业财务因素分析能力 • 具备企业非财务因素分析能力
	1－3 制定综合营销方案	• 能全面了解金融产品 • 具备产品组合能力 • 能制定个性化服务方案 • 掌握经济法常识
	1－4 与客户进行推销与定价谈判	• 懂得社交礼仪 • 具备表达、沟通能力 • 掌握营销、谈判技巧 • 能进行简单产品定价
	1－5 撰写调查报告	• 具备应用文写作能力
	1－6 后续服务	• 具有团队营销和交叉销售的理念
	1－7 营销方案的调整	• 具备行业发展前瞻性评估能力 • 具备捕捉企业经营状况变化的能力 • 具备金融服务方案的安全调整能力 • 能对前期营销成果进行总结
	1－8 客户关系维护	• 能分析客户需求 • 能设计客户维护方案 • 能提供金融咨询服务 • 能妥善处理客户投诉
2. 个人金融业务	2－1 客户识别	• 能制定渠道计划 • 能收集目标客户资料 • 能现场识别客户 • 能通过客户资料信息识别客户
	2－2 客户关系建立	• 能对客服关系进行定位 • 能促成客服关系 • 能掌握相关法律知识

续表

工作项目	工作任务	职业能力
	2－3 客户关系维护	• 能分析客户需求 • 能设计客户维护方案 • 能提供金融咨询服务 • 能妥善处理客户投诉
	2－4 产品营销	• 能对金融产品进行独立分析 • 能制定理财规划 • 能采集金融信息 • 能与客户良好沟通 • 能组织营销活动

（三）业务管理

工作项目	工作任务	职业能力
1. 资产业务管理	1－1 授信业务管理	• 能掌握授信业务种类 • 能掌握授信业务权限 • 能掌握授信业务执行标准 • 能掌握客户分类标准 • 能评定客户信用等级 • 能掌握相关业务政策法规 • 能进行企业财务分析 • 能了解产品定价方法 • 能了解风险资产的评估与风险系数的测定方法
	1－2 资金业务管理	• 能掌握资产负债管理原理 • 能掌握资金管理原理 • 能划分资金成本 • 能分析资金头寸 • 能掌握相关业务政策法规 • 能掌握资金管理权限
2. 负债业务管理	2－1 公司存款	• 具备基本的金融职业道德修养 • 具有一定的交际能力 • 了解银行会计结算业务流程 • 了解银行基本的资产业务、负债业务及中间业务，便于为公司客户量身定制理财计划

续表

工作项目	工作任务	职业能力
	2－2 个人存款	• 能掌握并熟练运用银行理财产品，为个人客户制定合适的理财计划 • 能与客户良好沟通
	2－3 同业存款	• 具备基本的金融职业道德修养 • 了解银行及非银行金融机构的相关情况 • 熟悉银行的优势产品吸引同业存款
3. 中间业务管理	3－1 理财顾问	• 能与客户沟通，具备良好的语言表达能力 • 熟悉金融法律、法规、政策 • 熟悉各项投资领域 • 能分析客户风险状况 • 能分析客户财务状况 • 能分析客户财务需求 • 能提供客户财务问题解决方案 • 能制定理财规划
	3－2 结算业务管理	• 能熟练掌握结算业务操作管理 • 具备良好的职业判断能力 • 能掌握结算业务操作风险控制方法 • 熟悉相关法律法规规定
	3－3 银行卡业务管理	• 能正确回收卡片 • 能根据会计要求平账、记账 • 能定期进行账务的检查 • 能初步审核申请文件的完整性和准确性 • 能初步掌握信用卡的授信等级 • 能基本识别信用卡风险 • 了解信用卡风险催收的基本方式 • 能根据客户的要求，准确完成临柜的服务工作 • 能根据业务管理及操作的要求，回答客户的问题，化解投诉 • 能运用 VIP 客户服务技能提供优质的高端客户服务 • 能根据不同的客户对象进行网点的产品营销
	3－4 担保类业务管理	• 熟悉相关的法律法规 • 具备良好的职业判断能力

续表

工作项目	工作任务	职业能力
		• 能正确办理银行承兑汇票、银行保函、跟单信用证、备用信用证等业务 • 能按银行授信标准判断客户风险 • 能分析客户风险状况 • 能分析客户财务状况 • 能对担保类客户进行风险管理 • 能正确处理担保业务纠纷
	3－5 票据业务管理	• 熟悉相关的法律法规 • 具备良好的职业判断能力 • 能正确执行银行内部关于票据管理规定 • 能理解票据行为特征 • 能正确进行票据操作 • 能辨别票据真伪 • 能处理票据纠纷 • 能正确进行票据清算
	3－6 代理代办及其他	• 熟悉相关的法律法规 • 具备良好的职业判断能力 • 能正确执行银行内部关于代理业务管理规定 • 能正确签订代理合同 • 能理解银行代理业务中的权利义务 • 能正确操作代理各项业务 • 能正确进行代理业务收费 • 能运用法律规范解决代理业务纠纷 • 能营销代理业务

五、培养目标

本专业人才培养的基本目标为：热爱祖国，拥护党的基本路线，遵纪守法，适应社会发展和区域经济建设需要，面向商业银行一线业务岗位，具有诚信、合作、敬业的职业素质，具备银行一线临柜交易、客户服务营销、业务管理的基本素质与操作技能，知识、能力、素质“三位一体”，德育为先，工学结合，知行合一，且具有一定可持续发展能力的复合型、发展型、高素质技术技能型金融应用人才。

六、人才规格

本专业毕业生应具有以下职业素养、专业知识、技能、能力和职业证书。

（一）职业素养

1. 思想政治素质：热爱祖国，拥护党的基本路线，掌握马列主义、毛泽东思想和中国特色社会主义理论体系的基本原理，有正确的人生观、价值观、道德观和法制观；

2. 人文与科学素质：具有科学精神和科学思维习惯，有健康、高雅的艺术与审美修养，有国际视野与跨文化理解能力，有较强的集体主义精神和鲜明的个性，并学有所长；

3. 身心素质：达到《国家学生体质健康标准》，养成良好的健身与卫生习惯，掌握一定的竞技运动和职业体育技能，具有积极向上的态度、良好的人际关系和健全的人格；

4. 专业伦理与职业道德：符合诚实信用、守法合规等专业伦理要求和勤勉尽职、公平竞争、专业胜任、保护商业秘密与客户隐私等职业道德要求，具有良好的职业态度、职业修养和终身学习能力，具有爱岗敬业、团队合作等职业精神，严格遵守相关法律法规，具有勤奋、严谨的职业习惯，具有较强的工作热情。

（二）专业知识

1. 掌握经济金融的基本概念与基础理论；

2. 了解有关金融法律法规的基本规定；

3. 掌握商业银行个人储蓄业务的基本知识、核算要求与操作流程；

4. 掌握财务会计的基础知识、核算要求与操作流程；

5. 掌握银行会计业务的基本知识、核算要求与操作流程；

6. 掌握商业银行授信业务的基本知识、业务要求与操作流程；
7. 掌握个人理财业务的基本知识、业务规范与操作规程；
8. 掌握互联网金融的基本知识；
9. 掌握金融营销的基本策略与营销技巧；
10. 了解商业银行风险管理的基本概念与基础理论；
11. 了解国际金融业务的基本概念、基础理论与相关的业务要求；
12. 掌握金融服务礼仪的基本规范与具体要求；
13. 了解证券投资业务的基本概念、基础理论与相关的业务要求；
14. 了解保险业务的基本概念、基础理论与相关的业务要求；
15. 掌握必需的、实用的英语知识；
16. 掌握一定的计算机和互联网知识。

（三）技能

1. 能准确快速进行手工点钞与机器点钞；
2. 能准确进行假币鉴别及现金挑残；
3. 能熟练使用五笔输入法打字；
4. 能熟练进行数字键盘的传票录入；
5. 能进行重要凭证、印章的盘点与入库；
6. 能准确进行账簿的登记与账目核对；
7. 能准确进行利息计算。

（四）能力

1. 具备柜面业务处理能力，能从事个人储蓄业务处理岗、现金出纳业务处理岗、对公结算业务处理岗、银行卡业务处理岗等岗位工作；

2. 具备授信业务处理能力，具有较强的分析、判断和决策能力，能够担任授信业务客户经理岗；

3. 具备理财规划能力，理解银行、保险、证券的关系，能够担任理财客户经理岗；

4. 具备商业银行风险识别和评估、控制能力，能够主动进行风险防范；

5. 具备产品营销能力，能够推销金融产品；

6. 具备较强的沟通、服务与应变能力，能快速妥善处理客户投诉；

7. 具备基层营业网点管理能力，能进行现场管理，快速分流和引导客户，指导客户使用自助设备，冷静处理突发事件；

8. 关注互联网金融行业发展动态，具备互联网思维能力；

9. 能在相应岗位上进行外语交流；

10. 能利用计算机录入数据、处理文档、查阅资料等。

（五）职业证书

本专业毕业生应取得证书包括：

1. 银行业专业人员职业资格证书；

2. 反假货币上岗资格证书；

3. 会计从业资格证书；

4. 全国高等学校计算机课程水平考试一级证书；

5. 全国高等学校英语应用能力考试三级/B 级证书。

鼓励学生取得证券从业人员资格证书、期货从业人员资格证书、国家理财规划师资格证书、信贷分析师资格证书、风险管理师资格证书、金融英语专业证书等职业资格证书。

七、课程体系框架

本专业的课程体系包括公共课程、专业课程、社会实践、毕业设计四个部分。其中专业课程包括专业基础课程、专业核心课程和专业选修课程。专业核心课程是根据专业培养目标而专门设置的课程，旨在培养学生的专业核心能力；专业选修课是学校结合自身的办学特色和专业方向而自行开设的课程，旨在培养学生在本专业某些特定领域内更具体的专业技能。社会实践包括专业认知实训、校内仿真实训、校外毕业实习。鼓励学生利用寒暑假时间开展社会调查活动，提高学生认识社会和服务社会的能力。

本专业学生在校期间完成的总学分应不低于 135 学分。

课程体系框架：

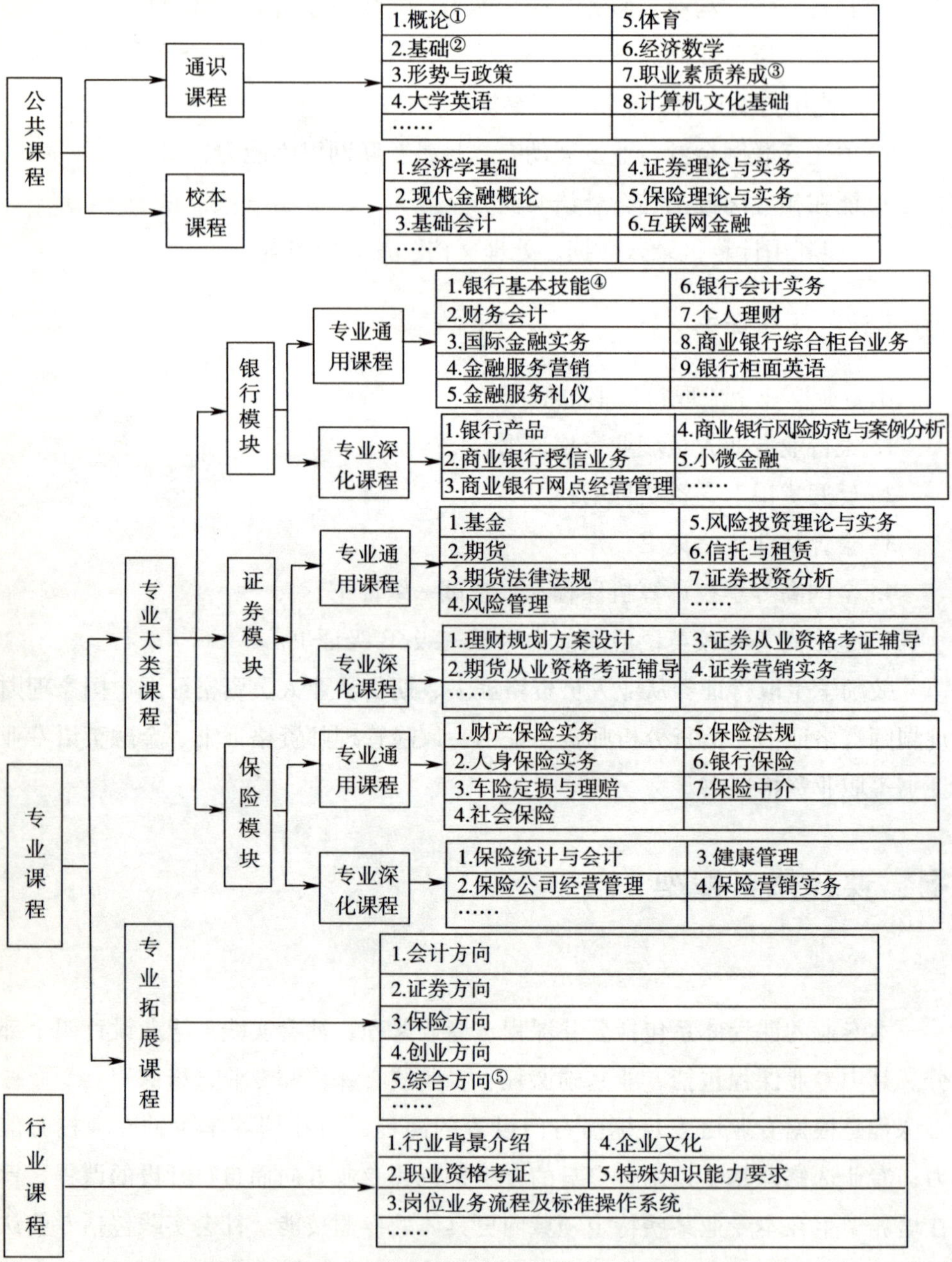

注：①《毛泽东思想和中国特色社会主义理论体系概论》简称《概论》；

②《思想道德修养与法律基础》简称《基础》；

③职业素质养成课程包括诚信文化理论与实践、高职学生学习生活指导、高职学生心理健康教程、高职学生职业生涯规划与就业指导、中国优秀传统文化等课程内容；

④银行基本技能课程包括中文五笔输入、电脑传票输入、点钞技术、反假货币技术；

⑤综合方向涉及会计、证券、保险、创业等多个方向。

八、课程设置

（一）基本素质课程

基本素质课程主要培养学生树立科学的世界观、人生观、价值观、道德观和法制观，提升人文和科学素养，养成良好的职业道德和职业发展能力。基本素质课程包括思想道德素质类课程、基本职业应用能力类课程、身心健康类课程。

本专业学生必须完成的基本素质课程包括概论、基础、形势与政策、大学英语、计算机文化基础、体育、经济数学、人文素质与职业素养。

（二）职业能力课程

职业能力课程是在对本专业学生必备的专业知识和专业技能进行分析的基础上系统设计的体现本专业职业要求的课程，包括职业通用能力课程、职业专门能力课程和职业拓展能力课程。

1. 职业通用能力课程

职业通用能力课程是根据完成岗位工作任务和学生职业发展对专业理论知识的需要而开设的，能够帮助学生更好地理解岗位工作，旨在培养学生基本的专业理论素质，是学生职业发展的基础。

本专业学生必须完成的职业通用能力课程包括现代金融概论、经济学基础、会计基础、证券理论与实务、保险理论与实务、互联网金融。

2. 职业专门能力课程

职业专门能力课程是为培养学生完成岗位工作任务所应具备的专门能力而开设的，旨在培养学生的专业核心能力。这类课程通过训练学生熟练地运用专门技术而达到使学生具备从事职业岗位工作基本能力的目的。

本专业学生必须完成的职业专门能力课程包括三个模块：银行模块、证券模块和保险模块。

（1）银行模块课程包括银行基本技能（包括点钞、五笔中文输入、电脑传票以及本外币反假等）、商业银行综合柜台业务、财务会计、个人理财、银行会计实务、国际金融实务、金融服务营销、金融服务礼仪、银行产品、商业银行授信业务、商业银行风险防范与案例分析、商业银行网点经营管理、小微金融。

（2）证券模块课程包括基金、期货、证券投资分析、风险投资理论与实务、信托与租赁、风险管理、期货法律法规、理财规划方案设计、证券营销实务。

（3）保险模块课程包括财产保险实务、人身保险实务、车险定损与理赔、社会保险、保险法规、保险公司经营管理、保险中介、银行保险、保险统计与会计、保险营销实务、健康管理。

3. 职业拓展能力课程

职业拓展能力课程是在学生掌握本专业必备知识和技能的基础上根据就业方向和个人发展需要所开设的选修课程。

本专业的职业拓展能力课程包括会计方向、证券方向、保险方向、创业方向和综合方向（涉及会计、证券、保险、创业等多个方向）五个方向。

（三）综合能力课程

综合能力课程是对上述课程所训练的能力综合运用的课程，包括社会实践和毕业设计。

1. 社会实践

本专业应注重培养学生的实践能力、调研能力和创业能力，教学方案中应组织相应的实践教学环节。实践教学组织包括专业认知实训、校内仿真实训、校外毕业实习。

（1）专业认知实训

专业认知实训是在专业课学习之前的一个实践教学环节，是指通过组织学生到商业银行、保险公司、证券公司等金融行业企业进行认知学习，培养学生对本专业的良好专业兴趣，从而树立正确的职业观。实训完成后，要有专业认知实训报告。

（2）校内仿真实训

校内仿真实训是指在部分专业课程，如商业银行综合柜台业务、商业银行授信业务、商业银行会计实务、银行卡业务、商业银行服务营销、商业银行服务礼仪等授课过程中开展操作训练。通过银行工作环境、银行业务凭证、银行印章、银行专用仪器设备、银行业务操作软件系统、票据票证鉴别仪器和软件等的仿真应用，强化学生对专业技能的学习与掌握，使学生具备运用银行专业技能进行规范服务与银行业务处理的能力。

(3) 校外毕业实习

校外毕业实习是实践性的教学环节，是指通过组织学生到商业银行、保险公司、证券公司等金融行业企业进行专业对口实习，培养学生适应社会、综合运用所学理论解决实际问题的能力。实习过程要有完整的实习记录，实习完成后要有实习报告，字数不少于2000字。

2. 毕业设计

毕业设计是本专业人才培养方案的重要教学环节，也是培养学生理论联系实际及提高学生研究性学习能力的有效手段。本专业的毕业设计应与毕业实习岗位相结合，毕业设计应强调应用性、实用性、可操作性及时效性。学生在修完所有规定课程后，必须完成一篇不少于4000字的毕业设计。经答辩委员会认定合格后，方可取得毕业证。

九、专业教学团队

本专业的生师比应不超过16:1，要组建一只高素质的“双师结构”教学团队，专任教师的“双师”比例达90%以上。专业核心课程应由校内专任专业教师和行业兼职教师共同完成教学。其中，实践实训部分应以行业兼职教师指导为主，行业兼职教师人数所占比例应不低于全部教师人数的50%。

1. 专任教师任职条件

具有高校教师资格证书；具有相关岗位工作经历或实践经历，熟悉银行业务，精通本专业的基本理论与知识；具有较强的教学与科研能力。

2. 兼职教师任职条件

具有5年以上相关岗位的工作经历；具有中级以上专业技术职务和本专业相关的职业资格，具有良好的教学组织能力。

十、教学安排

本专业教学安排应坚持学历教育与岗位培训相结合、职业能力与职业素质相兼顾、就业导向与人生发展相统一的原则。实施弹性学分制，逐步减少必修课，扩大选修课，增加学生学习选择权。要在完善第一课堂的基础上，着力构建与第一课堂有机衔接的第二、三课堂素质教育体系，通过校内、校外等系列活动或实践，促使学生完善自我，勇于竞争。

“三课堂”融合的专业教学安排如下图所示：

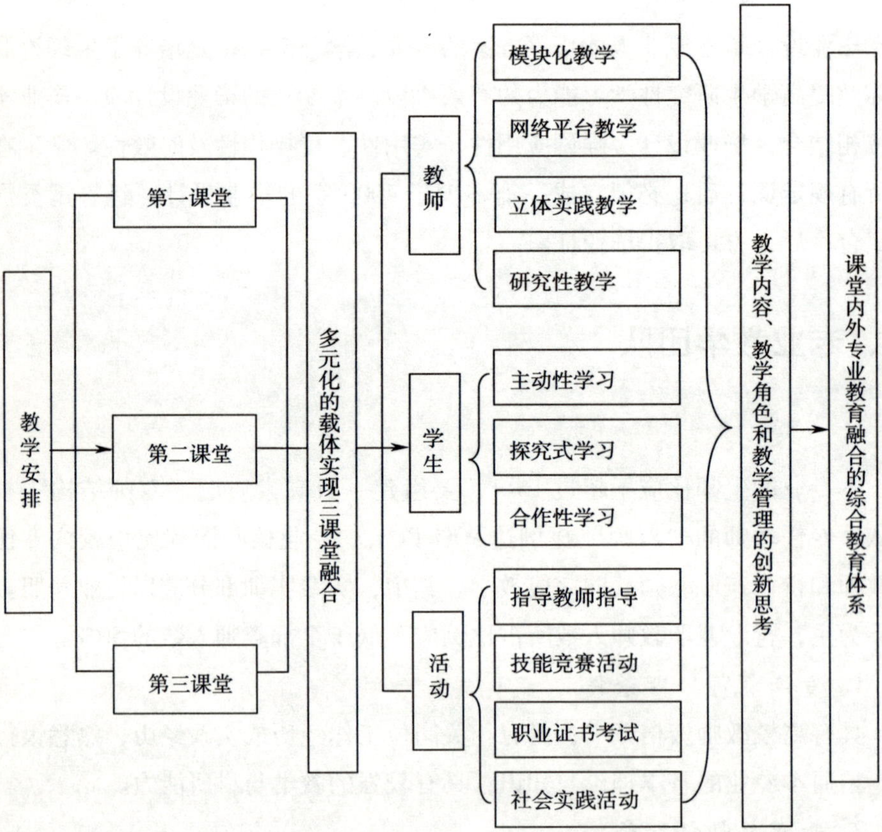

本专业教学安排可分为三个阶段：第一学年主要学习公共基础课程，并利用寒、暑假期进行专业认知实习，通过对金融机构、金融业务进行了解、接触，培养学生的专业基础能力；第二学年主要学习专业基础课程和专业核心课程，并利用寒、暑假期进行专业实习，通过统一安排与自行联系相结合的方式，安排学生进入金融企业、非金融企业财务资金部门进行岗位接触与业务操作，培养学生的专业基础能力和综合素质；第三学年主要面向行业企业，依据金融行业订单班与学生就业意向，安排学生进入银行一线个人储蓄、现金出纳、会计结算、银行卡、客户经理等岗位进行顶岗实习，实现“工学结合”，培养学生的职业能力，从而对接专业岗位，实现人才培养目标。

十一、教学条件

（一）教学设施

基于培养能熟练进行银行柜台业务操作的高素质技术技能型金融应用人才的目标，校企应共建全真型校内实训基地和紧密型校外实习基地，为学生开展银行业务实训、毕业实习提供基本教学条件。

在校内实训基地建设方面，应建立理论实践一体化的校内专业实训室，为学生提供一个身临其境的银行业务实训操作平台，满足学生对银行柜员岗位业务内容进行学习与实训的需要，提高其对银行柜员业务岗位的适应能力；为银行从业人员的业务培训提供服务，推动教学内容与教学方法改革。校内实训基地要能够实现对学生金融职业素养、金融文化礼仪、金融业务流程、金融业务技能等方面的职业能力的培养和训练。在校内实训基地的建设过程中，要密切与各商业银行实务部门的实践教学联系，实训内容、实训用具与教学软件资源配备要充分体现高度仿真性，设计、开发或购置银行业务处理过程所需的实训操作软件、仿真银行业务印章和业务凭证，配备点钞机、捆钞机、票据打印机、指纹仪、密码器等银行专业设备，以保障校内学生规模实训的有效开展。

要积极与金融企业开展产学合作，建设紧密型校外实习基地，以利于“工学结合”、毕业实习等教学活动的开展。建立网络教学平台，能够通过现代信息技术手段开展教学，专业核心课程均应具有能够通过网络教学平台与学生实施教学互动的功能。

1. 本专业应当配备的校内仿真实训基地

<table>
<tr><th rowspan="2">序号</th><th rowspan="2">实训室名称</th><th rowspan="2">实训项目</th><th colspan="2">设备配置要求</th><th rowspan="2">实训室规模</th></tr>
<tr><th>主要设备名称</th><th>数量</th></tr>
<tr><td rowspan="13">1</td><td rowspan="13">金融操作技能实训室</td><td rowspan="13">1. 假币和假证鉴别
2. 点钞
3. 汉字输入
4. 数字书写
5. 计算机速算
6. 小键盘输入
7. 设备操作
8. 票据填写及装订</td><td>多媒体教学设备</td><td>1 套</td><td rowspan="13">以 50 人为标准教学班配置</td></tr>
<tr><td>点钞机</td><td>13 台</td></tr>
<tr><td>假币鉴别设备</td><td>13 台</td></tr>
<tr><td>世界各国主要币种样品</td><td>51 套</td></tr>
<tr><td>算盘（选购）</td><td>51 把</td></tr>
<tr><td>计算器</td><td>51 个</td></tr>
<tr><td>凭证装订设备</td><td>13 台</td></tr>
<tr><td>打印机</td><td>4 台</td></tr>
<tr><td>传真机</td><td>4 台</td></tr>
<tr><td>复印机</td><td>4 台</td></tr>
<tr><td>扫描仪</td><td>4 台</td></tr>
<tr><td>电脑</td><td>51 台</td></tr>
<tr><td>点钞练习券、实训练习题、银行业务原始凭证</td><td></td></tr>
<tr><td rowspan="10">2</td><td rowspan="10">金融营销技能实训室</td><td rowspan="10">1. 有效沟通
2. 客户拓展
3. 金融产品销售
4. 金融服务礼仪</td><td>电脑</td><td>52 台</td><td rowspan="10">以 50 人为标准教学班配置</td></tr>
<tr><td>录音电话及传输控制设备</td><td>51 部</td></tr>
<tr><td>多媒体教学设备</td><td>2 套</td></tr>
<tr><td>网络打印机</td><td>1 台</td></tr>
<tr><td>服务器及网络设备</td><td>1 套</td></tr>
<tr><td>电话呼叫席位</td><td>51 套</td></tr>
<tr><td>录音笔</td><td>6 支</td></tr>
<tr><td>客户关系管理软件</td><td>1 套</td></tr>
<tr><td>网络营销平台</td><td>1 套</td></tr>
<tr><td>礼仪训练音像资料</td><td>1 套</td></tr>
<tr><td rowspan="3">3</td><td rowspan="3">银行柜台业务实训室</td><td rowspan="3">1. 本外币储蓄
2. 银行卡
3. 对公业务</td><td>电脑</td><td>51 台</td><td rowspan="3">以 50 人为标准教学班配置</td></tr>
<tr><td>服务器及网络设备</td><td>1 套</td></tr>
<tr><td>网络打印机</td><td>1 台</td></tr>
</table>

续表

序号	实训室名称	实训项目	设备配置要求		实训室规模
			主要设备名称	数量	
		4. 代理业务 5. 结算业务 6. 前台账务处理 7. 日初及日终处理	票据打印机	1台	以50人为标准教学班配置
			扫描仪	1台	
			商业银行综合柜台业务软件	1套	
			银行卡管理系统及读写设备	51套	
			多媒体教学设备	1套	
4	信贷业务实训室	1. 客户关系管理 2. 信贷业务管理 3. 信贷风险管理 4. 信贷资产管理 5. 信贷核算管理业务	电脑	51台	以50人为标准教学班配置
			服务器及网络设备	1套	
			网络打印机	1台	
			票据打印机	1台	
			扫描仪	1台	
			商业银行信贷业务软件	1套	
			多媒体教学设备	1套	
			全套业务原始凭证		
5	个人理财业务实训室	1. 建立和管理客户关系 2. 分析和诊断客户财务状况 3. 熟悉和开展银行、证券、保险、实物理财业务 4. 运用理财软件设计综合理财方案 5. 理财方案的实施和后续服务	电脑	51台	以50人为标准教学班配置
			服务器及网络设备	1套	
			网络打印机	1台	
			模拟理财产品	典型产品	
			模拟客户资料	典型客户	
			理财业务软件	1套	
			多媒体教学设备	1套	
			合同文本、单据、原始凭证		

2. 本专业应当配备的校外实习基地

序号	企业类型	数量	功能	接纳学生规模
1	商业银行/村镇银行	6	1. 训练学生从事银行柜台业务处理的能力 2. 训练学生从事银行理财产品营销和理财规划的能力 3. 训练学生从事营业现场管理和服务的能力	100
2	小贷公司	6	1. 训练学生从事信贷业务处理的能力 2. 训练学生分析问题、判断问题的能力 3. 训练学生客户管理的能力 4. 训练学生风险管理的能力	50

序号	企业类型	数量	功能	接纳学生规模
3	互联网金融公司	4	1. 训练学生熟悉互联网金融业务 2. 训练学生从事互联网金融业务处理的能力 3. 训练学生拓展网络客户的能力	50
4	其他企业	4	1. 训练学生从事收银业务的能力 2. 训练学生从事会计核算、财务管理的能力 3. 训练学生从事企业管理部门内勤业务的能力 4. 训练学生从事产品营销、理财服务、项目评估、风险管理的能力	120

（二）学习资源

1. 课程基本资源

本专业基本资源应做到系统、完整，反映课程的教学理念、教学设计、课程资源配置和应用，是教学活动必需的核心资源，主要包括课程介绍、教学大纲、教学日历、教案或演示文稿、重点难点指导、作业、参考资料目录和课程教学录像等。

基本资源结构图

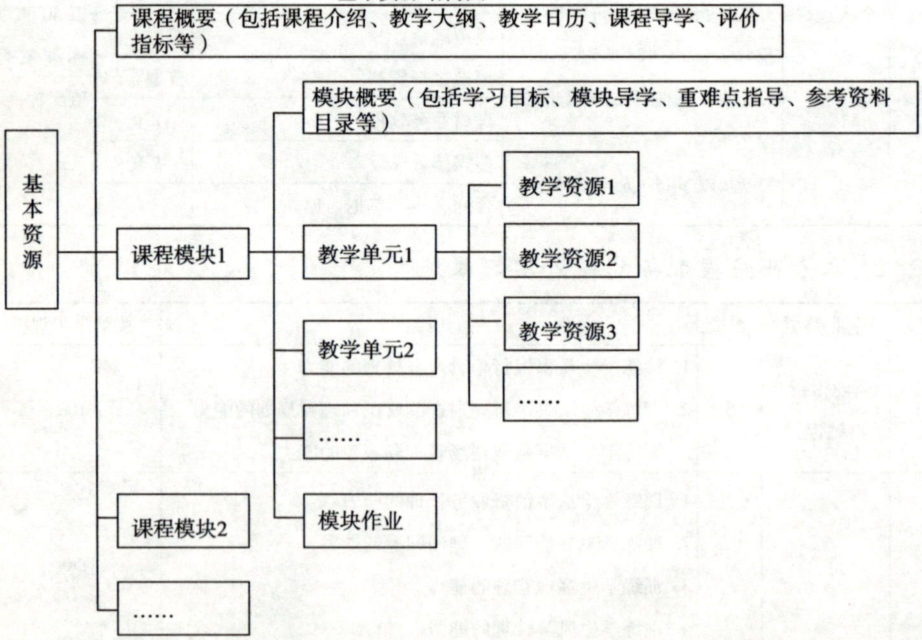

课程基本资源列表

序号	名称	格式要求	序号	名称	格式要求
1	课程介绍	Word	8	教学设计	Word
2	教学大纲	Word	9	课程录像	Mp4
3	教学日历	Word	10	典型案例	Word
4	重点难点	Word	11	习题试题	Word
5	电子教材	Word、ppt、视频文件	12	岗位介绍	ppt、视频文件
6	教学要求	Word	13	精彩问答	Word
7	教学课件	ppt	14	操作演示	ppt、视频文件

2. 课程拓展资源

本专业的拓展资源应反映课程特点，应用于各教学与学习环节，支持课程教学和学习过程，如案例库、专题讲座库、素材资源库，学科专业知识检索系统、演示/虚拟/仿真实验实训（实习）系统、试题库系统、作业系统、在线自测/考试系统，课程教学、学习和交流工具及综合应用多媒体技术建设的网络课程等。这些资源应实现线上线下有机结合。要配备与专业教学相关的、体现行业企业发展的新制度、新法规、新业务、新产品、新做法的图书资料、电子杂志等学习辅助性资源。课程的文档、图表、动画、视频、微课等基本资料应完全向学生开放，满足学生课下自主学习的需求。要结合专业发展的新趋势、人才市场需求的新变化、企事业用人单位的特定需求，及时进行教学资源与教学素材的调整、补充、更新，以满足培养市场化金融管理的专门人才的需求。

课程拓展资源列表

序号	名称	内容要求
1	在线课堂教学	教师能够对课堂教学活动自由设计，自由关联教学资源以及实训技能点，可以在教学中同步安排作业。
2	在线自主学习	学习者通过与教学资源的交互来获取知识，构建自己的知识体系模块。学生可以进行知识自测，教师可以监控学生的学习活跃度。
3	在线作业	教师可以通过布置作业、批阅作业、统计分析等随堂检验学生的学习效果。
4	在线考试	教师根据不同策略从题库中智能组卷或手工组卷，能够更加真实地考察学生的理论与实操能力。教师可以完成标准化考试自动阅卷和问答题人工阅卷，统计考试成绩。
5	在线交流问答系统	学生可以在线提出在学习过程中发现的常见问题，可以由教师进行问答，也可以由同学之间相互进行提问和回答，从而提高整体学习效率。

十二、教学方法

针对不同的课程，本专业应采取不同的教学手段与教学组织形式。

（一）理论课程

本类课程主要以案例教学形式为主，借助与当前学习主题相关的案例，引导学生带着任务和问题进入学习情境，使学习直观化和形象化，从而激发学生的主动性，促进知识的理解和运用。

1. 合作学习

可设定课程任务项目，引导学生主动去获取知识，并交由小组协作完成。鼓励学生对课堂所学提出自己的问题，鼓励其他学生为提问的同学解答，增强学生分析解决问题的能力和团队协作精神。

2. 角色互换

可选择个别章节作为学生自学、自讲、自评的内容，学生自己制作课件，小组成员进行协作，在课堂上讲授，其他小组成员和教师给予点评，使学生充分感受到学习的乐趣和师生之间的平等关系，提高教学效果。

3. “翻转”课堂

可借助现代教学技术和各种媒介，通过课堂讲授、课堂提问与讨论、课堂练习、最新资讯分析等教学手段实现教学课堂的“翻转”。

（二）技能类课程

技能类课程主要采用任务驱动型教学模式，根据临柜业务工作的需要，以行动为导向，开展一体化教学，使教师的讲授、示范与学生操作互动，学生提问与教师解答、指导相结合。让学生在“学”与“练”的过程中提高点钞技能、中文输入技能、电脑传票技能以及货币反假鉴别能力。

1. 示范教学

可以通过教师示范展示、观看实际操作录像等方法演示工作过程，进行直观教学。

2. 角色扮演

可划分为学习小组，每小组指定不同人员分别扮演银行柜员、存款客户、会计、企业客户等角色，模拟存款业务钞票清点、真假币识别、残币检出和兑换等业务办理过程，使学生体验不同角色的任务和职责。

3. 技能竞赛

可定期组织金融操作技能大赛，开展假钞识别、点钞速度、翻打传票、中文录入等技能竞赛，激发学生的竞争意识和训练的主动性。

（三）职业能力类课程

职业能力类课程实行项目教学、合作教学、任务驱动、案例教学、角色扮演、模拟教学、情景教学等多种形式的“做中学、做中教”的教学模式。教学过程中教师应积极引导学生提升职业素养，培养职业道德，实现知识、技能和态度的有机统一提升。

1. 项目教学

可在学生已掌握的知识、技能基础上，通过完成一定的“项目”巩固旧知识，获取新知识，提高学生学习的主动性、针对性和实用性，增强学生分析问题、解决问题的能力。

2. 情景模拟

可通过模拟真实工作场景训练学生技能。如客户拜访，可在角色扮演的基础上，模拟客户的办公环境，借助模拟情景，训练整个流程中所需的技能。

3. 真实情景练习

学生在完成模拟训练后，可安排学生到商业银行等校外实习基地，让学生在真实的工作场景下进行练习，通过行业人士评价和客户满意度调查检验学生各项技能的掌握程度。

4. 案例教学

案例教学法主要是借助一些客户开拓、产品推销等方面一些成功的案例，采用启发式、讨论式、研究式等生动活泼的教学方法，让学生在案例学习中提升职业能力。

十三、教学评价

（一）教师教学效果评价

本专业应建立学生评价、同行评价、督导评价和课程评价委员会评价相结合的评价体系，强化对教师的过程性监督。可从教学态度、教学内容、教学方法、教学效果四个方面对教师的教学效果进行评价。鼓励把课堂教学创新项目和相关奖励纳入到教学评价之中，多指标结合，建立合理有效的评价体系，对教师教学情况进行客观评价。

主要指标包括：

1. 教学态度重点考察教师按时上、下课，教学纪律，为人师表状况。

2. 教学内容重点评价教师讲授内容的科学性，对重点难点内容的处理和把握，教学信息容量，教材选择是否适合学生群体的层次。

3. 教学方法重点评判教师驾驭课堂的能力。教师讲解应深入浅出、重点突出、启发性强，教师应鼓励学生积极参与到课堂教学中，培养学生的学习兴趣和自主学习能力，引导学生进行研讨性学习和选择性学习。

4. 教学效果重点考察教师对于教学计划的完成情况、课堂气氛、学生分析问题解决问题的能力。教师要精心设计作业，并及时批改，发现学生学习中存在的问题，及时向学生反馈作业情况。

教师应具备现代信息技术运用能力、教学设计能力、教学资源开发与运用能力。教师应注重课程内容和教学方法的有机结合，灵活运用各种教学方法。鼓励教师自主创新教学方法，提高课堂教学的直观性，加强实践教学的可操作性，提升课堂教学实效。

（二）学生学习效果评价

对于学生学习效果评价方面，采用客观的定性评价与定量评价相结合、过程考核与结果考核相结合、校外评价与校内评价相结合的方法，改变以往期末考试一张试卷决定考核成绩的方式，采用多元化多维指标综合评定，突出对能力的考核评价方式，体现对综合素质的评价，逐步加大平时表现及平时实训成绩所占的比例，强调过程性学习，突出过程考核比重，从而增强学生的主体能力和学习主动性。

学习效果评价应包括学生的知识掌握情况、实践操作能力、学习态度和基本职业素质等方面。

1. 对于培养学生基本职业能力素养的专业基础能力实践课程系列，通过专门设计的操作考核标准系统进行客观评价，也可以通过以证代考、课证融合的方式进行课程评价，以期形成客观公正的评价指标体系，在标准化的评判机制下，达到学生职业能力提升的目的。

2. 对于专业核心能力实践课程系列，主要采用基于商业银行业务操作流程的项目化教学，在进行评价时将一张试卷定成绩的考试形式改为对学生的知识和能力相结合的综合素质进行全面性多视角评价的形式，侧重于学生对学习方法的掌握和综合能力的提高。如综合考虑课堂提问、学练结合、学生作业、平时测验、实验实训以及考试情况，过程考核和结果考核相结合，综合评定学生成绩。

3. 对于学生的专业实习教学环节评价，主要以实习企业评价为主，依据实习企业指导人士对学生知识、技能和学习能力、工作态度等实习情况的综合评定认定学生的专业实习成绩。

English Version

PREFACE

Vocational college education in China has entered a critical period of quality construction, which puts forward higher demand for the overall standardization and quality criteria of professional teaching. Meanwhile, financial institutions such as commercial banks have impose higher requirements for the comprehensive quality of frontline workers and systematic requirements for financial professional teaching. Therefore, developing professional teaching standards of world class and with Chinese characteristics for vocational education has become the key to improve China's vocational education quality and attraction.

By taking the work task analysis of commercial banks and other financial institutions as the starting point, the construction process of students' professional ability as the main line, the typical business process of frontline posts as the key units and elements, professional teaching standards of finance major establishes the overall framework of curriculum development, defines the curriculum contents, enhances the connection of academic certificate with professional certificates and of curriculum structure with professional ability structure of work posts, highlights the professionalism and practicability of curriculum system and solves the problem of curriculum teaching being out of line with professional ability requirements of industries and posts.

However, these standards are mainly structural and nominative professional construction requirements. They are only the basic professional ability requirements of finance major, which mainly regulate the relatively basic contents of this major. Therefore, these standards are open to modifications and other vocational colleges can use them as a basis for further development to adjust to their own needs.

Ⅰ. Program Name and Code

Financial Management and Practice (620103)

Ⅱ. Period and Diploma

Period of program: three years

Diploma: Junior College Degree

Ⅲ. Admission Requirements

High school graduates/Secondary vocational school graduates

Ⅳ. Career Development

Graduates will be qualified for conducting the front-line business in commercial banks and other financial institutions. The initial posts include counter service, product marketing, and business management, etc.

(Ⅰ) Counter Service

Work Categories	Tasks	Professional Abilities
1. Deposit taking; Counter teller service	1-1 Pre-opening preparation	• Carry out safety and sanitary inspection according to the rules • Get ready the equipments required for doing business according to the rules • Complete the handover of cashbox and prepare to start

续表

Work Categories	Tasks	Professional Abilities
	1-2 Customer reception and identification	● Communicate with customers effectively ● Examine the authenticity of customers' valid certificates ● Identify the authenticity of customers' payment documents such as certificates of deposit, bankbooks and cheques ● Confirm customers' signatures ● Know the specifications of all savings products (including deposit maturity, minimum amount of deposit, etc.) ● Comply to professional ethics
	1-3 Receiving and Paying out cash	● Know basic principles of receipt and paying out cash ● Be proficient in cash counting ● Accurately identify counterfeit money
	1-4 Keeping Accounts (Input)	● Examine and verify the conformity of certificate elements ● Be skilled in typing (Five-stroke input method) ● Be skilled in filling bank vouchers (by using numeric keyboard) ● Execute operations according to different business process specifications
	1-5 Re-checking (Authorization)	● Know relevant laws and regulations ● Be familiar with operational procedures ● Confirm customers' identity
	1-6 Business Processing at the End of the Day	● Be skilled in organizing various documents ● Carefully execute handovers such as the handover of cashbox ● Maintain a high level of risk awareness
2. Accounting service	2-1 Pre-opening preparation	● Carry out safety and sanitary inspection according to the rules ● Get ready the equipments required for doing business according to the rules. ● Sign up as a teller in the operation system
	2-2 Opening Accounts	● Master the basic knowledge of bank accounting ● Have a good understanding of the regulations of opening an account ● Know how to examine the materials for opening an account and check the authenticity and regulatory compliance of the relevant documents

续表

Work Categories	Tasks	Professional Abilities
		● Know how to fill out the account opening application form and ensure the completeness and accuracy of its information ● Be skilled in the operation of account opening and know how to execute it in the system
	2-3 Receiving and Examining bills	● Have a good knowledge of Payment and Settlement Measures and Law of Negotiable Instruments ● Distinguish the genuine bills from the counterfeit ● Know the basic standards of filling out the bills ● Know the needs of customers and keep good communications with them
	2-4 Keeping Accounts (Input)	● Be skilled with Chinese character input and input by using numeric keyboard ● Understand the regulations in Payment and Settlement Measures and Law of Negotiable Instruments. ● Know how to examine the authenticity of vouchers of various business bills such as bank drafts, commercial acceptance bills, transfer checks and summary documents, as well as the legitimacy of the elements on the bills ● Master basic accounting knowledge in banking business (accounting procedures, interest calculations and risk control) ● Master accounting operations in loan business and intermediary business ● Know the exchange rate and the regulations for capital settlement of the People's Bank of China ● Know the operation of input
	2-5 Re-check (Authorization)	● Be skilled with Chinese character input and input by using numeric keyboard ● Know the regulations in Payment and Settlement Measures and Law of Negotiable Instruments. ● Know how to examine the authenticity of vouchers of various business bills such as bank drafts, commercial acceptance bills, transfer checks and summary documents, as well as the legitimacy of the elements on the bills

续表

Work Categories	Tasks	Professional Abilities
		• Master basic accounting knowledge in banking business (accounting procedures, interest calculations and risk control) • Master accounting operations in loan business and intermediary business • Know the exchange rate and the regulations for capital settlement of the People's Bank of China • Have some knowledge and awareness of business risks • Know the operation of input
	2-6 Cancelling an Account	• Master the basic knowledge of bank accounting • Have a good understanding of the regulations of cancelling an account • Know how to examine the materials for cancelling an account and check the authenticity and regulatory compliance of the relevant documents • Master all examination procedures before account cancellation • Be skilled in the operation of account cancellation and know how to execute it in the system • Master Administrative Rules for RMB Bank Settlement Accounts and Payment and Settlement Measures issued by People's Bank of China
	2-7 Operations at the end of the working day	• Organize and check the business vouchers of the day • Take stock and put in storage of important bills and seals • Sign out the system correctly
3. Bankcards Service	3-1 Cash withdrawal at the Counter	• Have a good understanding of the function and fare standards of bankcards • Examine and verify bankcards in different categories, and identify fake cards • Verify the authenticity of customers' ID • Operate in the system following operational procedures • Master the operational rules for authorization of managers when authorization of higher level is needed and know how to operate • Check customers' signatures

续表

Work Categories	Tasks	Professional Abilities
	3-2 Deposit (Repayment) at the Counter	• Have a good understanding of the function and fare standards of bankcards • Be skilled in verifying the authenticity of banknotes and identifying counterfeit money • Operate according to business procedures
	3-3 Transfer at the Counter	• Have a good understanding of the function and fare standards of bankcards • Examine and verify bankcards in different categories, and identify fake cards • Verify the authenticity of customers' ID • Operate in the system following operational procedures • Master the operational rules for authorization of managers when authorization of higher level is needed and know how to operate • Check customers' signatures
	3-4 Account Cancellation at the Counter	• Identify the card type • Inquire and confirm in the system the unclosed services before cancelling an account and handle it according to the regulations • Carry out the execution of cancelling an account correctly in the system • Withdraw bankcards based on the requirements of risk control and complete related accounting treatment
	3-5 Report of the Loss at the Counter	• Deal with customers' loss reports of cards • Be skilled in dealing with loss-reporting operation
	3-6 Receiving bills at the Counter	• Check the correctness of bills according to business rules • Verify the accuracy of the amount in the bills • Conduct bill receiving operation correctly
	3-7 Inquiring and modifying customers' data	• Handle the customers' requirements • Operate in the system correctly
	3-8 Dealing With Application Forms	• Examine and verify the completeness and accuracy of the application form • Make initial judgment of the credit line to be applied according to the credit rating

续表

Work Categories	Tasks	Professional Abilities
	3-9 Customer Complaints and Consultation	• Handle customers' complaints according to relevant business management rules • Handle customers' enquiries according to relevant business management rules
	3-10 ATM Reset (Excluding Clearing)	• Be skilled in ATM reset procedures and be able to perform correctly • Operate cash dispenser of an ATM correctly • Deal with usual shutdowns of an ATM
	3-11 Special Service	• Renew bankcards upon requests and operate according to the rules • Adjust temporary credit limits of credit cards according to credit extension policy • Freeze and thaw a bank card according to the requirements of risk management

(Ⅱ) Service Marketing

Work Categories	Tasks	Professional Abilities
1. Financial services for enterprises	1-1 Identifying targets of marketing	• Know the present situations of different industries • Be particularly familiar with at least one industry
	1-2 Investigating customers' profiles and their positions in the industry	• Be able to analyze the companies' positions in the industry • Have the ability to analyze the financial factors of one company • Be able to analyze non-financial factors of one company
	1-3 Making marketing plans	• Have a comprehensive understanding of financial products • Have the ability to design financial products combination • Have the ability to provide personalized services • Have a basic knowledge of economic law
	1-4 Negotiating with customers on sales and pricing	• Know social etiquette • Have the ability to communicate effectively with customers • Master marketing and negotiating skills • Know how to price financial products

续表

Work Categories	Tasks	Professional Abilities
	1-5 Writing investigation reports	• Know how to write business reports
	1-6 Follow-up services	• Know how to do team marketing and cross-selling
	1-7 Making adjustment to marketing plans	• Have the ability to make prospective assessments about the development of an industry • Have the ability to identify the changes in the state of an enterprise • Have the ability to make adjustments to financial service plans • Have the ability to make summaries about previous marketing outcomes
	1-8 Maintaining customer relations	• Be able to analyze customers' needs • Be able to design customer relation maintenance plans • Be able to provide financial counselling services • Be able to deal with customer complaints
2. Financial services for individuals	2-1 Identifying potential customers	• Be able to make plans about potential customer channel • Be able to collect information about potential customers • Be able to identify potential customers on the working site • Be able to identify the customers through customer information database
	2-2 Building customer relations	• Be able to classify the customer relation • Be able to facilitate customer relations • Know related laws
	2-3 Maintaining customer relations	• Be able to analyze customers' needs • Be able to make customer maintenance plans • Be able to provide financial counselling service • Be able to deal with customer complaint
	2-4 Marketing products	• Be able to make independent analysis about financial products • Be able to make financial planning • Be able to gather financial information • Be able to communicate effectively with customers • Be able to organize marketing activities

(Ⅲ) Business management

Work categories	Tasks	Professionalabilities
1. Assets Management	1-1 Loan business management	• Know the types of loan business • Master the limits of authority of loan business • Master the access criteria of loan business • Master the standards of customer classification • Be capable of evaluating customers' credit rating • Know related policy and regulations • Be capable of analyzing corporate finance • Know product pricing methods • Understand the methods of capital-at-risk evaluation and risk coefficient measurement
	1-2 Fund business management	• Master the principles of asset-liability management • Master fund management theory • Be capable of classifying fund cost • Be capable of analyzing fund position • Know related policy and regulations • Master the limits of authority of fund management
2. Liability management	2-1 Company deposit	• Comply to basic financial ethics • Have necessary communicative ability • Understand the process of settling accounts in bank accounting business • Understand the asset, liability and intermediary business, so as to make tailored financial plans for company customers
	2-2 Individual deposit	• Proficiently marketing bank finance products, so as to make tailored finance plans for individual customers • Be able to communicate effectively with customers
	2-3 Financial institutions' deposit	• Comply to basic financial ethics • Know the situation of banks and other financial institutions • Be familiar with bank competitive products, thus drawing financial institutions' deposit

续表

Work categories	Tasks	Professionalabilities
3. Intermediary business	3-1 Financial consultant	• Be able to communicate well with customers and be qualified with good language expression ability • Be familiar with financial laws, regulations and policies • Be familiar with each investment field • Be capable of analyzing customers' risk status • Be capable of analyzing customers' financial situation • Be capable of analyzing customers' financial demands • Be able to offer solutions to solve customers' financial problems • Be able to make financial plans
	3-2 Settlement management	• Master settlement management • Have a good ability of professional judgment • Master risk control of settlement operation • Be familiar with related laws and regulations
	3-3 Bank cards business management	• Be able to withdraw cards correctly • Be capable of balancing and keeping accounts according to accounting requirements • Be able to check accounts regularly • Be able to preliminarily examine and verify the application papers to make sure the information is filled in completely and correctly • Preliminarily know the credit ratings of credit cards • Be able to basically identify the risks of credit cards • Understand the basic ways to collect credit card payment • Accomplish counter service according to the requirements of the customers • Be able to answer customers' questions and solve complaints according to business management and operation requirements • Be able to offer VIP services to high-end customers • Be able to market and sell products to different customers according to their different profiles
	3-4 Guarantee business management	• Be familiar with profiles related laws and regulations • Have a good professional judgment ability

续表

Work categories	Tasks	Professionalabilities
		• Be capable of dealing with bank acceptance bills, letters of guarantee, documentary letters of credit, standby letters of credit and so on • Be capable of assessing customers' risks according to credit extension standards • Be capable of analyzing customers' risk status • Be capable of analyzing customers' financial situations • Be able to manage risks for guarantee business customers • Be able to solve guarantee business disputes
	3-5 Bill business management	• Be familiar with related laws and regulations • Have a good professional judgment ability • Comply to bank rules about bill management • Understand the traits of bill activity • Conduct bill activity correctly • Be able to distinguish the genuine bills from the forged ones • Be able to solve bill business disputes • Be capable of clearing bills
	3-6 Agency business and others	• Be familiar with related laws and regulations • Have a good professional judgment ability • Comply to agency business rules made by the bank • Conclude and sign agency contract correctly • Understand the rights and duties of bank agency business • Carry out agency business correctly • Collect agency business fees correctly • Be able to solve agency business disputes under legal framework • Be able to market agency business

V. Educational Goals

This program aims at cultivating graduates who should love our country, support our party, observe the disciplines and obey our law, and who are to meet the needs of social development and regional economic development. Directed to serve the frontline business of commercial banks, our graduates should have the professional qualities of integrity, cooperation and dedication as well as the fundamental quality and operational skills required by over-the-counter transaction, customer service marketing and business management. By forming a "trinity" of knowledge, ability and quality, prioritizing moral education, integrating work and study, and combining knowledge and action, this major aims to cultivate versatile, highly adaptable, higly-qualified, highly-skilled professionals with sustainable development ability.

VI. Graduate Qualifications

Graduates should have professional quality, knowledge, skills and abililty. They should also acquire certain professional certificates.

(I) Professional Quality

1.1 Ideological and Political quality

Graduates should love their country and support the basic line of the Communist Party. Having good understanding of the principles of Marxism-Leninism, Maoism and theoretical system of Chinese socialism, they should have correct philosophy, value, morality and awareness of law.

1.2 Humanistic and scientific quality

Students should have scientific spirit and thinking logic. They should have healthy and elegant artistic and aesthetic sense. They should have global vision and cross-cultural understanding. The graduate should also have a strong spirit of collectivism, a distinguishable personality and specialized knowledge.

1.3 Physical and mental health

Graduates should meet the requirements of national student physical health standard and have bodybuilding and hygienic habits. They should master a certain competitive sports and professional sports skills. They should have positive attitudes, good interpersonal relationships and healthy personalities.

1.4 Professional ethics and morality

Graduates should conform to the requirements of professional ethics such as honesty, credibility, law-abiding and regulation compliance, the requirements of professional moralities such as diligently fulfilling one's duty, fair competition, professional competence and protecting business secrets and customer privacies. They should have good attitudes, professional quality and lifelong learning ability. They should have professional spirits of dedication and team cooperation, attitudes of strictly obeying laws and regulations, habits of diligence and preciseness and a strong passion for work.

(Ⅱ) Professional Knowledge

2.1 Understand concepts and principles of finance and economics;

2.2 Be familiar with financial laws and regulations;

2.3 Have the fundamental knowledge, accounting requirements and operation procedure of personal savings business of commercial banks;

2.4 Have the fundamental knowledge, accounting requirements and operation procedure of financial accounting;

2.5 Have the fundamental knowledge, accounting requirements and operation procedure of bank accounting business;

2.6 Have the fundamental knowledge, business requirements and operation procedure of loan business of commercial banks;

2.7 Have the fundamental knowledge, business regulations and operation procedure of personal finance business of commercial banks;

2.8 Have the fundamental knowledge of internet finance;

2. 9 Have the basic strategy and marketing skills of financial marketing;

2. 10 Understand the basic concepts and fundamental theories of risk management of commercial banks;

2. 11 Understand the basic concepts, fundamental theories and related business requirements of international financial business;

2. 12 Know the basic regulations and specific requirements of financial service etiquette;

2. 13 Understand the basic concepts, fundamental theories and related business requirements of securities investment business;

2. 14 Understand the basic concepts, fundamental theories and related business requirements of insurance business;

2. 15 Know the basic and practical English;

2. 16 know the use of computer and internet.

(Ⅲ) Skills

3. 1 Be able to do manual counting and machine counting of banknotes accurately and fast;

3. 2 Be able to identify counterfeit money and pick out worn banknotes;

3. 3 Be proficient in Chinese character input by using five-stroke input method;

3. 4 Be proficient in voucher input by using numeric keyboard;

3. 5 Be able to check important vouchers and seals and put them in storage;

3. 6 Be accurate in the registration of accounting books and the check of accounts;

3. 7 Be accurate in calculating interests.

(Ⅳ) Abilities

4. 1 Have the ability of dealing with on-the-counter business and be competent in posts of personal savings business, cash depositing and withdrawing business, non-private settlement business and credit card business;

4. 2 Have the ability of dealing with loan business. Have a strong ability in analysis, judgment and decision-making and be competent in the post of credit

business customer manager;

4.3 Have the ability of financial planning. Be able to understand the relationship between banks, insurance companies and security companies and be competent in work post of wealth manager;

4.4 Have the ability of identifying, assessing and controlling commercial bank risks and be able to actively take prevention measures;

4.5 Have the ability of product marketing and be able to promote financial products;

4.6 Have a strong communication, service and contingency dealing ability and be able to deal with customer complaints quickly and properly;

4.7 Have the ability of managing branches and be able to implement field management, quickly distribute and guide customers, instruct customers to use self-service equipments and calmly deal with emergencies;

4.8 Focus on the developmental dynamic of internet finance and have internet thinking ability;

4.9 Be able to communicate in English;

4.10 Be able to input data, process documents and search information on computers.

(V) Certificates

Graduates should acquire the following certificates:

Certification of China banking professional

Certificate of qualification in anti-counterfeit notes

Certificate of accounting professional

Common computer test level 1 for national college students

CET 3/ PRETCO-B

Certificates students are encouraged to acquire:

The qualification certificate for security professionals

The qualification certificate for futures professionals

National financial planner qualification certificate

Credit analyst qualification certificate

Risk manager qualification certificate

Financial English certificate

Ⅶ. Curriculum System

Our curriculum system includes general courses, major courses, social practice and graduation project. Major courses include basic major courses, core major courses and selective major courses. Major core courses are designed for our educational goals that focus on developing students' professional core abilities. Selective major courses are designed to cater to our college-specific features and major fields, with the goal of helping students get more knowledge and skills in specific areas. Social practice includes professional cognitive training, intra-college simulative trainings and pre-graduation internships. We also encourage students to make good use of their summer and winter vacations to participate social investigation, which improves students' ability of knowing and serving the society.

The minimum requirements of credit hours for graduation are 135.

Curriculum system:

Compulsory Curriculum → General Education Curriculum →

1.Introduction ①	5.Physical Education
2.Foundations②	6.Economic Mathematics
3.Situation and Policy	7.Ethics③
4.College English	8.Foundation of Computer Science
……	

Compulsory Curriculum → Core Curriculum →

1.Fundamental Economics	4. Securities
2.Fundamental Finance	5. Insurance
3.Fundamental Accounting	6.Internet Finance
……	

Postscript:

①*Introduction* is an abbreviation for *introduction to Mao's Philosophy*;

②*Foundations* is an abbreviation for *Foundations of Moral Standards and Basics of Law*;

③The professional ethical curriculum includes: *Professional Ethics and Practices*, *Study Instructions for Higher Vocational Students*, *Mental Health for Higher Vocational Students*, *Career Instructions for Higher Vocational Students* and *Chinese Traditional Virtues*;

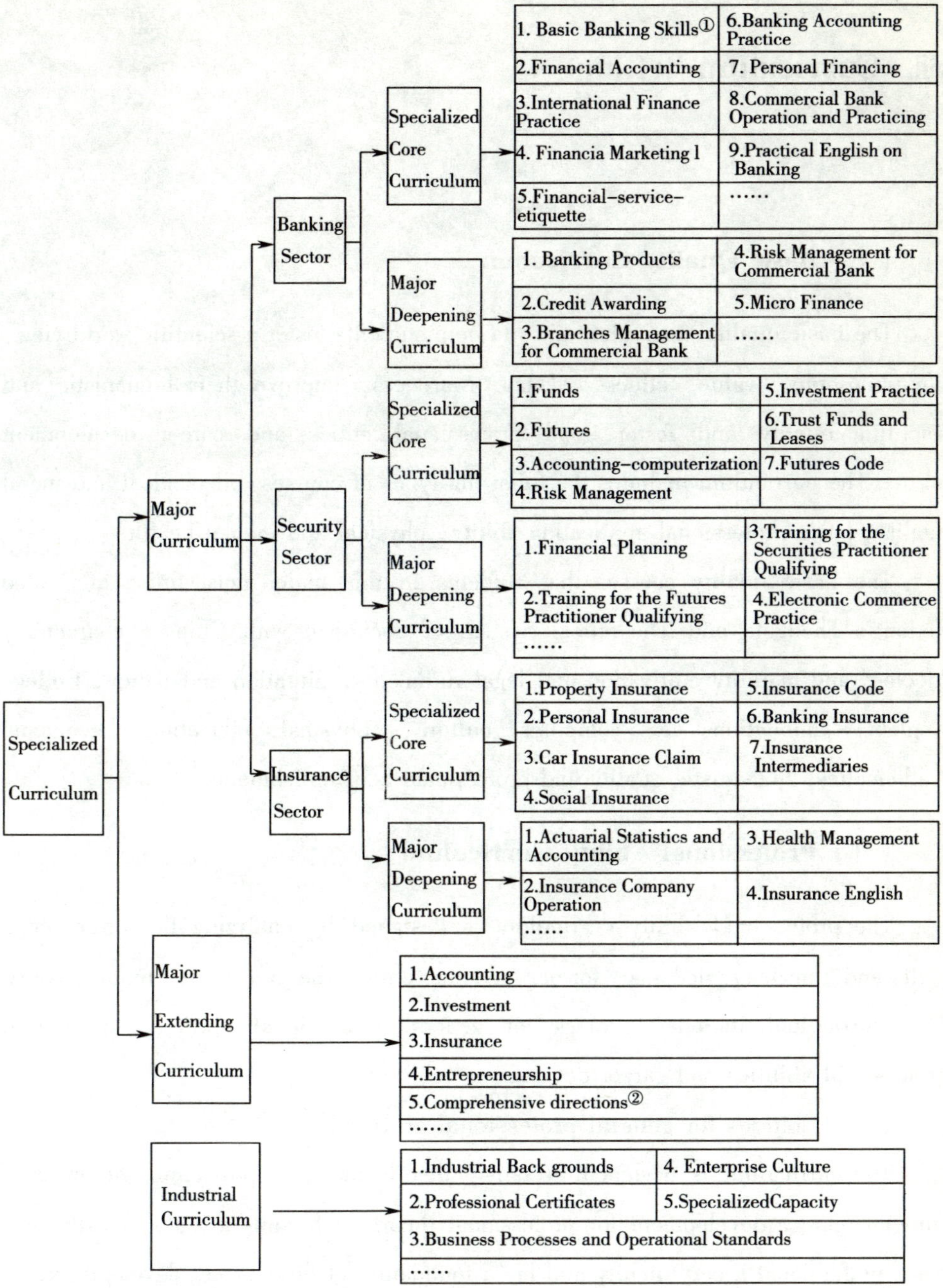

Postscript:

①The basic banking skill curriculum includes *Chinese Typing*, *Bank Vouchers Typing*, *Money Counting and Anti-counterfeit Currency*.

②Comprehensive directions can be related to accounting, investment, insurance and entrepreneurship.

Ⅷ. Curriculum Setting

(Ⅰ) Basic Quality Curriculum

The basic quality curriculum aims to help students foster a scientific world view, life philosophy, value, ethics and law awareness, improve their humanistic and scientific quality and foster good professional ethics and career development ability. The curriculum includes the following types of courses: ideological and moral quality, basic professional application ability, physical and mental health.

The basic quality courses that students in this major must finish are: Mao Zedong's Thoughts and Theoretical System of Socialism with Chinese characters; Ideology and morality cultivation and legal rudiments; Situation and policy, College English, foundations of computer culture, physical education, economic mathematics, humanistic quality and professional accomplishment.

(Ⅱ) Professional Ability Curriculum

The professional ability curriculum is designed by analyzing the professional skills and knowledge necessary for our students to meet the professional requirements. This curriculum includes courses for general professional abilites, specialized professional abilities and career development abilites.

2.1 Courses for general professional abilities

The curriculum is designed to satisfy the demands of posts and the need of students' career development for professional theories. It aims to cultivate students' basic professional theory quality and lay a foundation of their career development.

The courses for general professional abilities that students must accomplish are: Introduction to Modern Finance, Fundamental Economics, Fundamental Accounting, Securities Theory and Practice, Insurance Theory and Practice, and Internet Finance.

2.2 Courses for specialized professional abilities

Courses for specialized professional abilities are set up to develop students' core ability of accomplishing tasks. Students will be trained to deftly use the specialized techniques, thus having the ability of working on professional posts.

Courses for specialized professional abilities that students must accomplish include three modules: bank, securities and insurance.

2.2.1 Bank module courses include basic banking skills (such as cash counting, Chinese input with Five-stroke input method, processing vouchers on PCs, identifying counterfeit foreign and domestic currencies and so on), general counter business of commercial banks, financial accounting, personal finance, bank accounting business, international finance business, financial service marketing, financial service etiquette, bank products, loan business of commercial banks, risk prevention and case study of commercial banks, management of commercial bank outlets, SME finance, etc.

2.2.2 Securities module courses include investment analysis of funds, futures and securities, risk investment theory and practice, financial trust and leasing, risk management, regulations and laws on futures, design of financing planning, and securities marketing practice.

2.2.3 Insurance module courses include property insurance practice, life insurance practice, car damage assessment and claim settlement, social insurance, insurance regulations, insurance company management, insurance intermediary, bank insurance, insurance statistics and accounting, insurance marketing practice and health management.

3. Courses for career developmental abilities

Career development courses are set up according to students' future career direction and individual development requirement. Students will take the courses after they master the fundamental professional knowledge and skills.

Career development courses include Accounting, Security, Insurance, Entrepreneurship and the mix of the above.

（Ⅲ）Comprehensive Ability Courses

Comprehensive Ability Courses, which include social practice and graduation project, are the comprehensive mix of the above courses and skills.

1. Social Practice

This major highlights importance of cultivating students' practical, research and entrepreneur ability, with practical teaching procedures included in the courses. Practical teaching includes professional cognitive training, intra-college simulation training and graduation internship.

（1） Professional cognitive training

Professional cognitive training starts before professional curriculum. We will organize students to visit financial institutions, such as commercial banks, insurance companies, securities companies and so on. The goal is to develop students' interest in this major and help them build up right profession concept. Students should hand in professional cognitive training reports after training.

（2） lntra-college simulation training

lntra-college simulation training refers to the operational training especially for courses such as general counter business of commercial banks, credit granting business of commercial banks, banking accounting practice, bank card business, service marketing of commercial banks, and service etiquette of commercial Bank. It is beneficial for students to master professional knowledge after simulation of banking setting, bank business vouches, bank seals, specialized bank equipments and devices, operation and processing software system of bank business, and note identification equipments. Students should be capable of providing standard services and dealing with bank business.

（3） Graduation Internship

Graduation internship is practical teaching process. We will organize students to carry out professional training in financial institutions, such as commercial banks, securities and insurance companies. Students will have an internship in these companies to improve their social ability and the ability of solving real problems through the use of theoretical knowledge. A complete internship record and report are needed for every student. Moreover, internship report should be over 2000 words.

2. Graduation Project

Graduation Project is the key part of talent training. It is also an effective way to improve students' ability of linking theory with practice and promote students' research and study ability. Graduation project of this major should be connected with internship. Applicability, practicability, operability and timeliness are the requirements of graduation project. After finishing all courses, student must hand in a graduation paper of more than 4000 words. Only after the graduation paper is affirmed as eligible by the graduation project committee can students get graduate certificate.

Ⅸ. Professional Teaching Team

The ratio between students and teachers should be less than 16:1. Moreover, to build a high quality teaching team, double-qualified professional teachers should account for 90 percent of all full-time teachers. Core professional courses should be taught together by full-time professional teachers and part-time teachers from industry. Part-time teachers who have rich experience in related industry should play a key role in practical training, of which part-time teachers ought to count up no less than 50 percent of all teachers.

1. The necessary qualifications for becoming a full-time teacher are: acquiring University Teacher Qualification Certificate, having experience in related industry, being familiar with bank business, being proficient in fundamental theories and knowledge of finance, and having good research and teaching ability.

2. Part-time teachers should be qualified with rich experience in related industry (over 5 years), at least mid-level technical position, related professional certificate and very good teaching ability.

X. Teaching Arrangement

Teaching arrangement should adhere to the principles of linking academic education with on-the-job training, giving due consideration to both professional ability and qualities simultaneously, and integrating employment with personal develoment. It is necessary to have more flexibility, gradually reduce compulsory courses, and increase elective courses so that students have more options on learning. Apart from mastering the booklore, students will benefit a lot from quality teaching system which connects book learning with after-class study closely.

Integrated "three chassrooms" arrangement

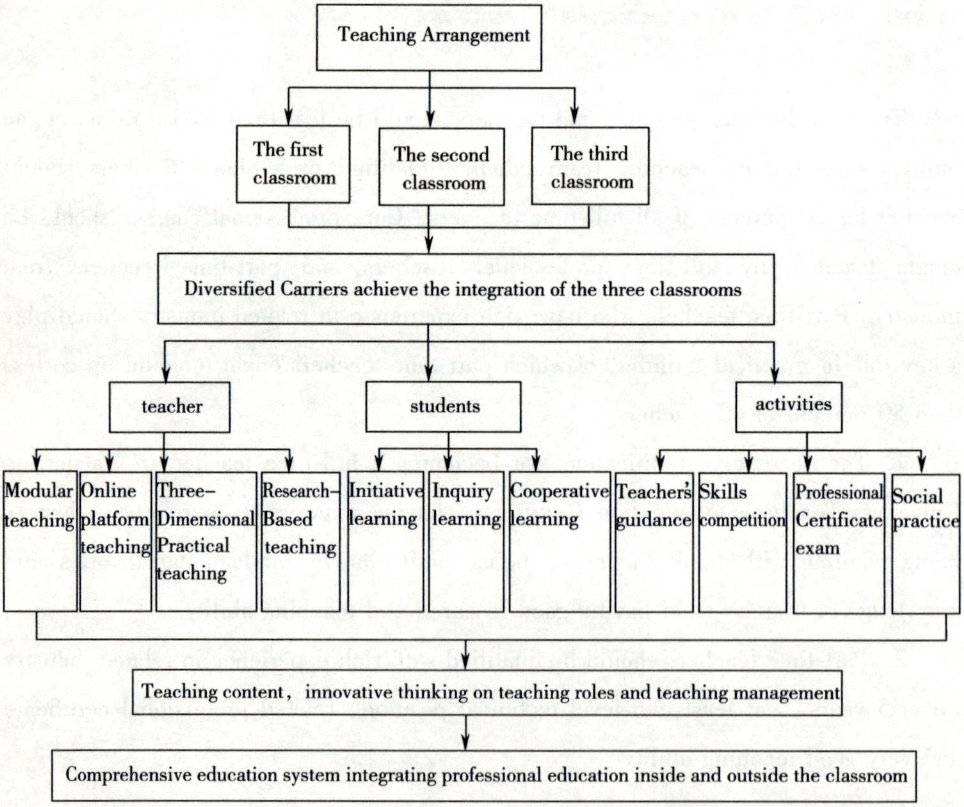

There are three stages of teaching. In the first year, students mainly focus on public basic courses. Besides, they will have professional cognitive practice during winter and summer vacations to understand and get in touch with financial institutions and financial business, thus cultivating their fundamental professional ability. During the second school year, students mainly learn fundamental professional courses and core professional courses. They will make use of winter and summer vacations to have professional internships in related industries. In the third year, students will study elective professional courses targeting at certain industry and enterprise. The graduate internship is linked to specific employment posts such as personal deposit, cash receiving and withdrawing, accounting, bank card business and customer manager, thus achieving the object of integrating working and study. We will encourage students to attend various activities, competitions and industry trainings based on their interests.

XI. Teaching Condition

(Ⅰ) Teaching Facilities

As our object is cultivating high-end talents with proficient skills for bank counter business, it is necessary for college and enterprises to work together on building up simulation training bases in campus and out of campus, thus offering places for students to practice bank business training and graduation internship.

To meet the demand of students' bank business practice and improve students' adaptive capacity, we should build up veritable practice classrooms which can be used both for booklore teaching and professional skills training. The classrooms can also be used by people who have already worked in banks, thus pushing teaching reform forward. Campus training base should help improve career qualities, financial culture manner, financial business process, financial business skills and so on.

Campus training base should be connected closely with bank business practice teaching. Moreover, content of training courses, equipments and teaching software should be in accordance with real setting in a bank. We will design or purchase bank business operation softwares as well as simulated seals and vouchers that are used in bank business. Cash-counting machine, banknote packing machine, certificate printer, fingerprinter machine, cipherer and so on should be equipped to guarantee the effect of training for all students on a large scale.

We cooperate actively with financial enterprises and set up off-campus training base, which is beneficial for integrating work with study and for graduate internship. By building up internet teaching system, teachers will be able to teach by using modern information techniques. Besides, all core professional courses should have interaction function with students through internet teaching system.

1. On-campus simulation training bases

<table>
<tr><th rowspan="2">No.</th><th rowspan="2">Training room</th><th rowspan="2">Training tasks</th><th colspan="2">Facility requirements</th><th rowspan="2">Training Capacity</th></tr>
<tr><th>items</th><th>Quantities</th></tr>
<tr><td rowspan="13">1</td><td rowspan="13">Financial operation skills training room</td><td rowspan="13">1. Identifying counterfeit currency and certificate
2. Money counting
3. Chinese characters typing
4. Numeric writing
5. Rapid calculation with computers
6. Keypad tying
7. Equipment operation
8. Bill filling and binding</td><td>Multimedia teaching facility</td><td>1</td><td rowspan="13">50 persons</td></tr>
<tr><td>Money counter</td><td>13</td></tr>
<tr><td>Currency verifier</td><td>13</td></tr>
<tr><td>Foreign currency samples</td><td>51</td></tr>
<tr><td>Abacus (optional)</td><td>51</td></tr>
<tr><td>Calculator</td><td>51</td></tr>
<tr><td>Voucher binding equipment</td><td>13</td></tr>
<tr><td>Printer</td><td>4</td></tr>
<tr><td>Fax machine</td><td>4</td></tr>
<tr><td>Copier</td><td>4</td></tr>
<tr><td>Scanner</td><td>4</td></tr>
<tr><td>Computer</td><td>51</td></tr>
<tr><td>Money counting practice notes、training exercises paper、original bank vouchers</td><td></td></tr>
</table>

续表

No.	Training room	Training tasks	Facilityrequirements items	Quantities	Training Capacity
2	Financial marketing skills training room	1. Efficient communication 2. Customer development 3. Financial products marketing 4. Financialservice etiquette	Computer	52	50 persons
			Dictaphone and transmission control facility	51	
			Multimedia teaching facility	2	
			Network printer	1	
			Server and network device	1	
			Calling equipment	51	
			Voice recorder	6	
			Customer relationship maintaining software	1	
			Network marketing platform	1	
			Etiquette training video	1	
3	Bank Counter services training room	1. Deposits in RMB and foreign currencies 2. Bank cards 3. Services for corporates 4. Agency services 5. Account settlements 6. Over-the-counter accounts operation 7. Settlements at the begin and the end of the day	Computer	51	50 persons
			Server and network device	1	
			Network printer	1	
			Bill printer	1	
			Scanner	1	
			Banking counter services software	1	
			Bank cards management system	51	
			Multimedia teaching facility	1	
4	Loan Services training room	1. Customer relations management 2. Loan services management 3. Loan risks management 4. Loan assets management 5. Loan accounting management	Computer	51	50 persons
			Server and network device	1	
			Network printer	1	
			Bill printer	1	
			Scanner	1	
			Commercial bank loan operation software	1	
			Multimedia teaching facility	1	
			Full set of original bank vouchers		

续表

No.	Training room	Training tasks	Facilityrequirements		Training Capacity
			items	Quantities	
5	Personal finance business trainingroom	1. Build and maintain customer relations 2. Analyze customer financial situations 3. Provide services related to banking, securities, insurances and financial planning 4. Make financial planning using investment software 5. Execute financial planning and provide follow-up services	Computer	51	50 persons
			Server and network equipment	1	
			Network printer	1	
			Simulated financial products	Typical products	
			Simulated customer information	Typical customers	
			Financial planning software	1	
			Multimedia teaching facility	1	
			Contracts, invoices, vouchers		

2. Off-campus training bases

Number	Types of Enterprise	Quantities	Functions	Capacity
1	Commercial Bank/ Village Bank	6	1. Training for the bank teller position 2. Financial products marketing and financial planning training 3. Service management training	100
2	Small-Sum Loan Companies	6	1. Loan service training 2. Analytical and judgment ability training 3. Customer management training 4. Risk management training	50
3	Internet Finance Companies	4	1. Training for students to get familiar with internet financial business 2. Training for students to deal with internet financial business 3. Training for students to develop online customers	50
4	Other enterprises	4	1. Training for the cashier position 2. Accounting and financial management training 3. Office work training 4. Marketing, financial service, project evaluation and risk management training	120

(Ⅱ) Learning Resources

1. Basic Resources for the courses

The basic resources for this major should be systematically complete, and should reflect the teaching philosophy, teaching design, and allocation and application of the courses. Basic resources form the core resource of the entire teaching activity. The resources range from course introduction, syllabuses, teaching calendars, lesson plans, presentation slides, guidance on both key points and difficulties, homework, references, teaching videos and other resources.

Structure of Basic Resources

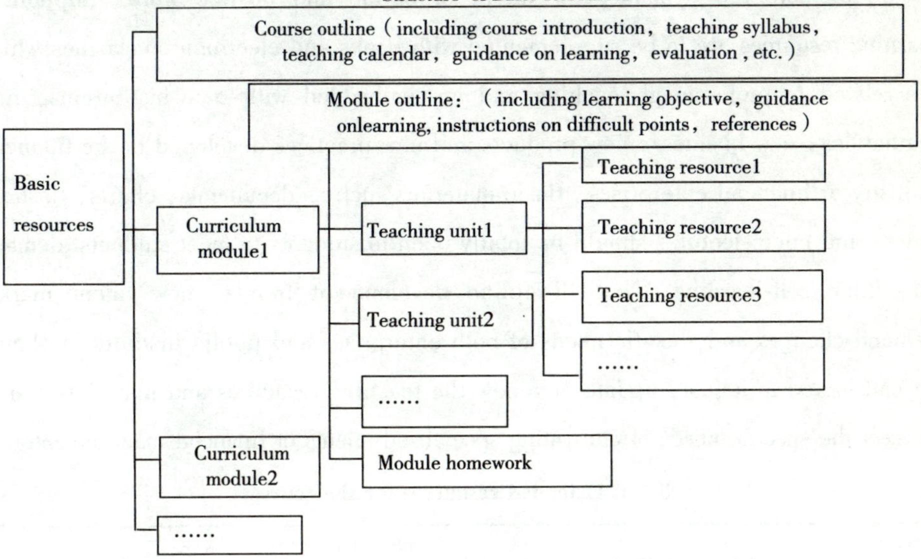

List of Basic Resources

No.	Designation	Format requirement	No.	Designation	Format requirement
1	Course introduction	Word	8	Teaching plan	Word
2	Teaching Syllabus	Word	9	Video	Mp4
3	Teaching calendar	Word	10	Study Cases	Word
4	Emphasis and difficulties	Word	11	Exercises and test	Word
5	Electronic learning material	Word, ppt, videos	12	Job introduction	ppt、videos
6	Teaching requirements	Word	13	Questions and answers	Word
7	Teaching courseware	ppt	14	Presentations	ppt、videos

2. Extended Resources For the Courses

The extended resources for this major should depict the features of the course, and should be applied to each teaching and learning stages, supporting the whole teaching and learning process. Extended resources cover the resources such as case data base, seminar libraries, material database, professional literature retrieval system, demonstrational/virtual/simulated experimental practical training (internship) system, examination database system, homework system, online self-testing/examination system, communication tools for teaching and learning, and online courses constructed on integral application of multimedia technologies. It should promote the dynamic integration of online and off-line work. Supporting learning resources are to be supplemented with books and electronic magazines which are related to professional teaching and are embedded with new institutions, new regulations, new business, new products and new practices developed in the financial industry or financial enterprises. Basic materials such as documents, charts, flashes, videos and micro-lectures should be totally open to students to meet students' demand for offline self-learning. New discipline development trends, new talent market demand changes and specific needs of both enterprises and public institutions should be considered to adjust, update or renew the teaching resources and materials, so as to meet the specific needs of cultivating specialized talents of financial management.

list of Extended resources for the course

No.	Name	Content Requirement
1	Online classroom teaching	Teachers can freely design teaching activities, link teaching resources with practical skillpoints and assign homework.
2	Online autonomous learning	Learners acquire knowledge and construct their own knowledge systemthrough their interaction with the teaching resources. Students can have knowledge self-test and teachers can monitor students' learning activeness.
3	Online homework	Teachers can test students' learning outcomes in class by assigning homework, checking homework and statistical analysis.
4	Online exam	Depending on different strategies, teachers can generate test papers from the test database either automatically or manually. The generated test papers can effectively evaluate students' theoretical ability and operational ability. Teachers can do automatic marking of examination paper and question-and-answer and do test score statistics.

续表

No.	Name	Content Requirement
5	Online question-and-answer system	Students can put forward common questions found in the learning process online. The questions can be answered by teachers or can be questioned and answered among students. Overall learning efficiency can be improved in this way.

XII. Teaching Methods

For different courses, different teaching methods and teaching-learning patterns should be adopted.

(I) Theoretical Courses

These courses is mainly based on case study. By studying the cases that are related to the current subject, the courses guide the students into a learning context with tasks and questions in their minds. By visualizing the learning project, students' motivations are inspiried and the understanding and using of the knowledge thus facilitated.

1. Cooperative Learning

Task projects can be set to guide the students to gain knowledge on their own initiatives, and the tasks should be completed through teamwork. Students should be encouraged to raise their own questions about what they have learned in class, and answer questions raised by other students. This will strengthen students' ability of analyzing and solving problems and improve their teamwork spirit as well.

2. Role Exchanging

Teachers can select some sections to be the materials for self-learning, self-presentation and self-evaluation. Students have the chances to make slides by themselves, deliver lectures by groups in class, and then receive comments from other group members and the teacher. By this way, the students can fully feel the pleasure of learning and the equal relationship between the teacher and the students, and the teaching effectiveness will then be improved.

3. Flipped Classroom

With the help of modern teaching technologies and other media, flipped classroom teaching mainly refers to using such teaching methods as delivering lectures, raising questions, organizing discussions, exercising, analyzing latest news.

(Ⅱ) Skill Courses

Skill courses mainly adopt task-driven teaching mode. Based on the needs of on-the-counter business and oriented towards actions, integrated teaching mode combines teachers' lectures and demonstrations with students' interaction, and combines students' questions with teachers' answers and instructions. This process of learning and practicing helps students improve the skills of money-counting, typewriting in Chinese, processing bank vouchers and identifying counterfeit money.

1. Demonstration Teaching

Display the working process by using methods such as teacher demonstration and presentation and students watching videos on practical operation.

2. Role Play

Divide students into several learning groups. For each group, let the students play different roles such as bank teller, depositor, accountant and corporate customer. Through practices such as imitating money-counting of the deposit business, identifying the banknotes, changing and picking out worn currency, the students are able to have a good understanding of the tasks and responsibilities of these positions.

3. Skill Competition

The college will organize financial operating skill competitions periodically, including counterfeit money identification contest, money-counting speed contest, sorting and typing vouchers contest, and Chinese character input contest as well. The competitions will stimulate students' competitive awareness and training initiative.

(Ⅲ) Professional Ability Courses

Professional ability courses follow the methods of project teaching, cooperative teaching, task-driven teaching, case study, role play, simulation teaching, on-site teaching and other forms of " learning in practicing, teaching in practicing" modes. Teachers should positively guide the students to improve their professional quality, cultivate their career ethics, and promote the integration of knowledge, skills and attitude.

1. Project Teaching

On the basis of students' existing knowledge and skills, a certain kind of projects can be used to consolidate the existing knowledge and gain new knowledge. This helps improve students' learning initiative, pertinence and practicability, and enhance students' ability of analyzing and solving problems.

2. Scenario Simulation

Train students' skills by guiding them to simulate real working scenarios. Scenario simulation, for examples, visiting customers can help train all the abilities required over the entire process, on the basis of role play and the simulation of customers' working environment.

3. On-site Practice

Students can be sent to off-campus practice base such as commercial banks after completing simulated training. They will practice what they have learned in the real working places. The comments they receive from industry veterans and customers' satisfaction survey are considered as a standard to test whether they have mastered the various skills.

4. Case-based teaching

By learning from some successful cases in the banking business fields such as customer development and product promotion, case-based teaching method is lively and active, which adopts heuristic method, discussion method and research method to develop students' professional ability.

XIII. Teaching Evaluation

(Ⅰ) Teaching Effectiveness Evaluation

This program should build an evaluation system of teaching quality composed of students' assessment, peer evaluation, supervisors' comments and Course Evaluation Committee's comments. Teaching effectiveness should be based on four aspects, that is, teachers' morality, course content, teaching method and teaching effect. Course teaching innovation project and related rewards should be encouraged to be included in teaching evaluation system. A reasonable and effective evaluation system with multi-index evaluation method should be built to assess teachers' teaching performance objectively.

The main indices included are:

1. Teacher's morality: start and dismiss class punctually; teaching discipline; being a model for students.

2. Teaching content: scientificity of teaching content; how to deal with and handle the difficulties and key points; richness of teaching information; whether teaching materials are suitable for students.

3. Teaching method: refers to the ability of teachers to manage the classroom. Teachers should explain profound knowledge in simple language and highlight to the key points. The teaching should focus on enlightening students. Encourage students to actively participate in teaching, cultivate students' learning interests and self-learning ability and promote discussion-based learning and selective learning.

4. Teaching effectiveness: focuses on teachers' completion of teaching plan, classroom atmosphere, students' ability of analyzing and solving problems. Teachers should design the homework carefully, correct homework timely, find out the problems in students' learning and give feedback to students' homework.

Teacher should have the ability of using modern information technology, teaching designing, development and application of teaching resources. Teachers should emphasize on the combination of course contents and teaching methods by using a variety of teaching methods freely. Teachers should be encouraged to bring forth new teaching methods, to improve the visualization of the lectures and to increase the operability of practical teaching, thus raising the effectiveness of teaching.

(Ⅱ) Students' Learning Effectiveness Evaluation

For the students' learning effectiveness evaluation, instead of using traditional pattern of assessing students by one final testing paper, we combine objective qualitative evaluation with quantitative evaluation, process assessment with result assessment, and off-campus assessment with in-campus assessment. An overall diversified multi-index assessment system should be employed to increase the proportion of students' daily performance and practical performance, which gives more weight to process assessment, so that students' ownership and initiatives are better reflected.

Students' learning effectiveness evaluation should include aspects such as to what extent the students have learned the knowledge, the ability of practical operation, learning attitude and fundamental professional qualities.

1. For the practical course series aiming at cultivating students' basic professional quality: Standard operation evaluation system is specially designed to give objective evaluation. What's more, the methods of replacing exams with certificates and integrating certificates with courses can be used for course evaluation. Thus, objective and fair evaluation index systems are formed and under standardized evaluation mechanism, and students' professional ability are improved.

2. For the practical course series aiming at improving students' core professional ability: Project teaching based on operation processes of commercial banks is adopted. In evaluation, the traditional pattern of assessing students on one final testing paper is replaced by comprehensive and multi-perspective assessment method which combines students' knowledge with their ability and focuses on students'

mastery of learning methods and improvement of their comprehensive ability.

3. For the evaluation of students' professional internship: Students' professional internship performance is comprehensively assessed mainly based on the evaluation of enterprises. Students' knowledge, skills and learning ability, work attitude will be evaluated by enterprises' tutors.